FREEDOM *to* READ

To all the educators who open our worlds to freedom
—L. C.-R.

To my mother, Arsine Cameron
—J. E. R.

SIMON & SCHUSTER BOOKS FOR YOUNG READERS
An imprint of Simon & Schuster Children's Publishing Division
1230 Avenue of the Americas, New York, New York 10020

Photo of Hampton University football team provided courtesy of the Hampton University Archives, Hampton, VA
Book design by Laurent Linn

The text for this book was set in Le Monde Courrier Std.
The illustrations for this book were rendered in watercolor and pencil.
Manufactured in China
0426 SCP
First Edition
2 4 6 8 10 9 7 5 3 1
CIP data for this book is available from the Library of Congress.
ISBN 9781534463509
ISBN 9781534463516 (ebook)

FREEDOM *to* READ

The Story *of* Teacher Mary Peake *and* One Mighty Oak Tree

WRITTEN BY
Lesa Cline-Ransome

ILLUSTRATED BY
James E. Ransome

A Paula Wiseman Book
SIMON & SCHUSTER BOOKS FOR YOUNG READERS
New York Amsterdam/Antwerp London
Toronto Sydney/Melbourne New Delhi

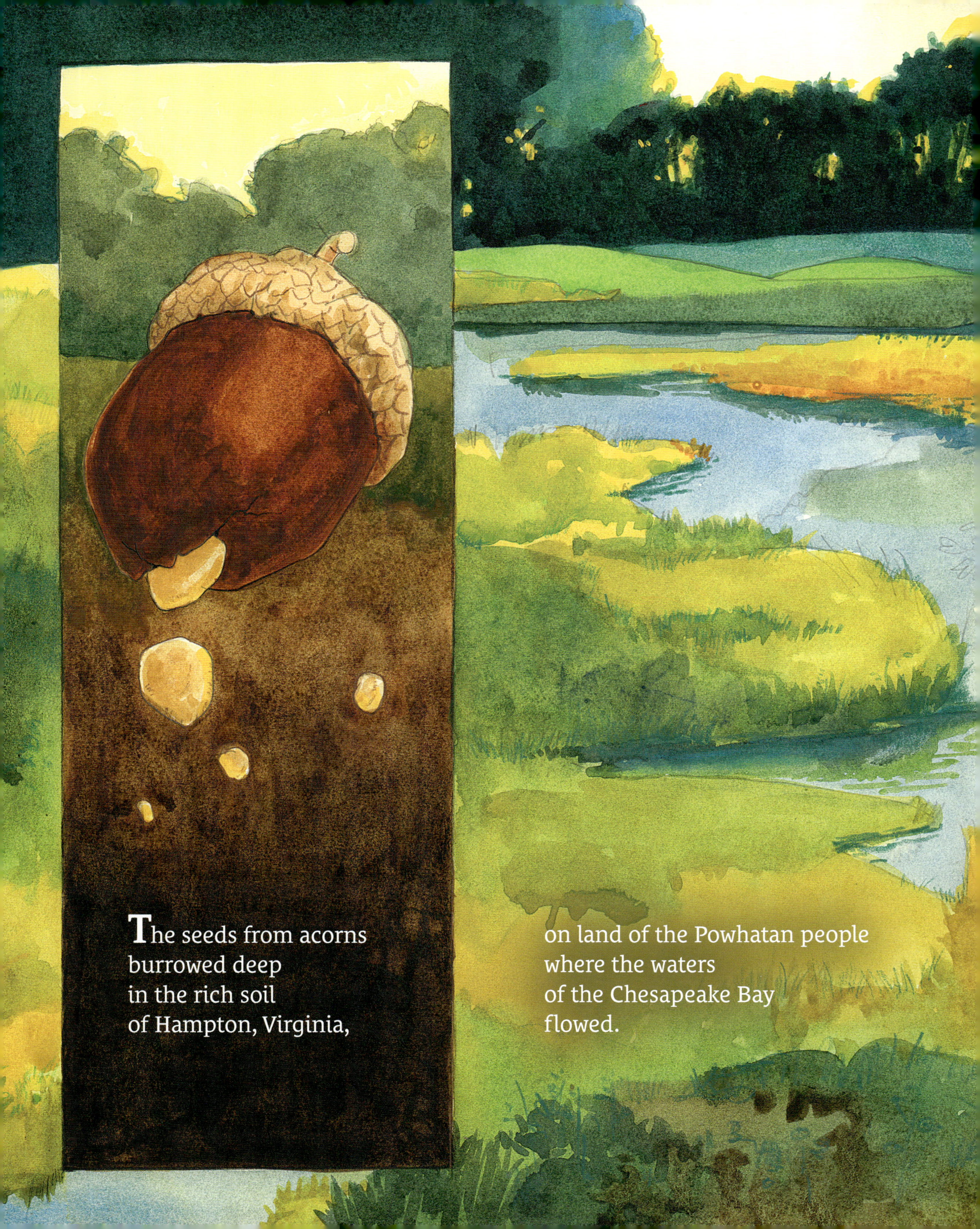

The seeds from acorns
burrowed deep
in the rich soil
of Hampton, Virginia,

on land of the Powhatan people
where the waters
of the Chesapeake Bay
flowed.

The seeds waited
for rain and sun,
hooves and paws
to trample them in tight.

Finally
one bright green leaf
sprouted
on a stem of an oak tree

that grew
into a trunk.

Its branches
flung wide open
like a hug,

strong,
proud,
mighty,
and **free**.

Free
from the bondage of slavery,
Mary Kelsey
was born
in 1823 in
Norfolk, Virginia,
to Sally,
a free colored mother.

Mary grew knowing
her Bible said
what the law did not.
All men are equal
in the eyes of God,
thought Mary.
The color
of skin
did not make
one man a master
over another.
Free as Mary was,
colored free
was not the same
as free
in **Virginia**.

Alexandria, **Virginia**,
became home
to Mary at six years old,
when Sally sent Mary off
to an aunt and uncle
and a colored school there.
Teachers treated her kindly.
Taught her
reading,
writing,
and arithmetic.
Dressmaking,
sewing,
and needlework.
I am blessed
in mind
and spirit,
Mary thought
as she savored her Bible
and rose
to the top of her class.
Her hunger for learning
made Mary
drink in her letters,
devour her numbers
down to their very last **drop**.

Dropped acorns
from the STRONG OAK
fed families of deer
and burrowing wild boar.
Robins gathered
its wispy moss
into homes
for nesting chicks.

One August eve
in 1831
the warm wind stilled.
In the air
was ***a rebellion***.

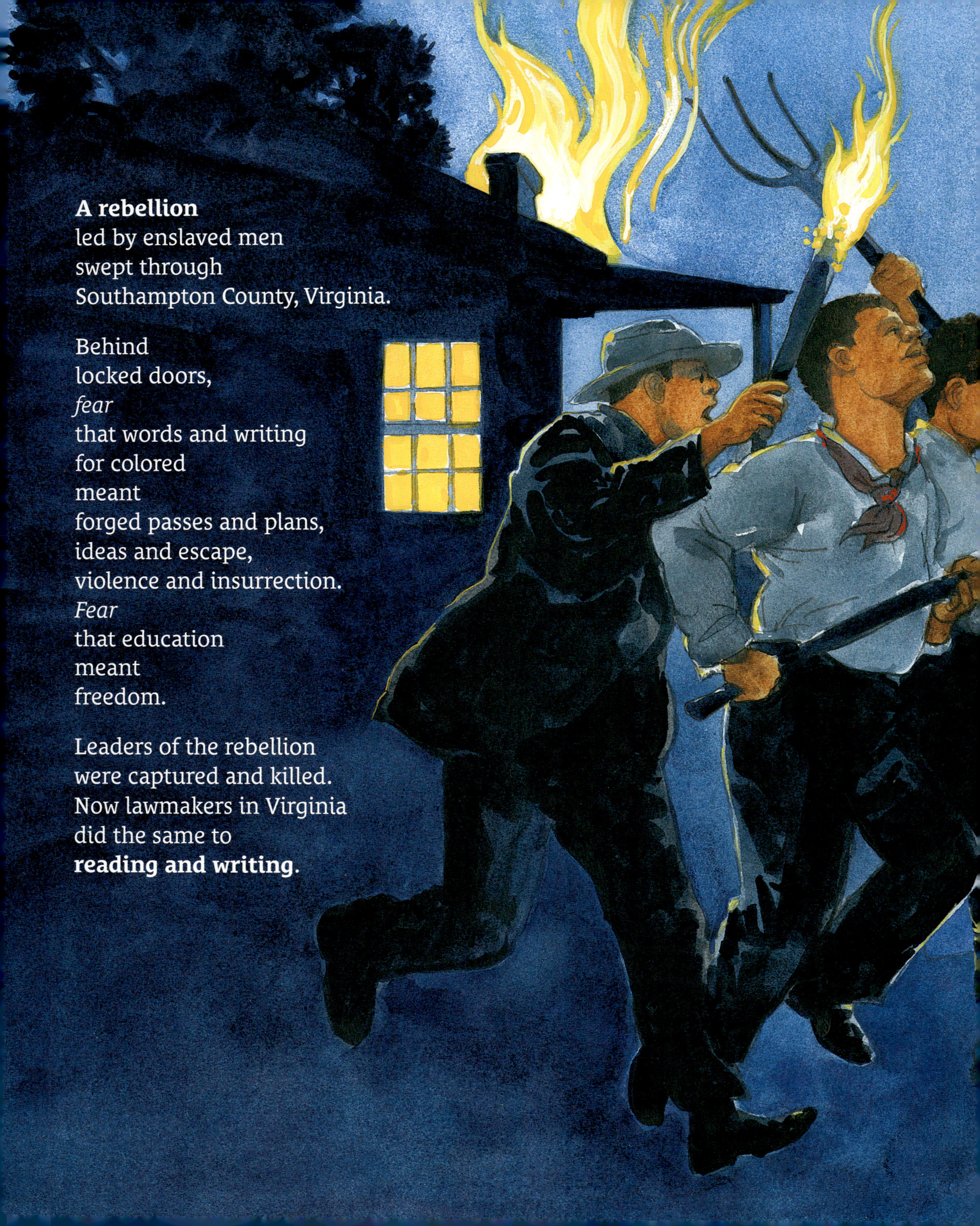

A rebellion
led by enslaved men
swept through
Southampton County, Virginia.

Behind
locked doors,
fear
that words and writing
for colored
meant
forged passes and plans,
ideas and escape,
violence and insurrection.
Fear
that education
meant
freedom.

Leaders of the rebellion
were captured and killed.
Now lawmakers in Virginia
did the same to
reading and writing.

Reading and writing
for colored,
enslaved and free,
ended in Virginia,
and education
became outlawed.
All the schools
closed their doors
by order of the state
in 1831.

Mary returned to Norfolk
a young woman of sixteen years,
still hungry
for education,
now starved
by law.

Mary began stitching together a life,
sewing
to earn her keep.

Her Bible told her to share
her gifts.
But how? Mary wondered.

When her mother married
Thompson Walker,
the three moved
to a new home
in Hampton
with a pretty front parlor
big enough
for guests,
church meetings,
club gatherings.
Mary knew then
it would also
be big enough
to share her gifts.

Firm as the earth
Thy gospel stands . . .
If I am found
In Jesus's hands,
Mary sang aloud
in praise.

Her parlor
would also
be big enough,
Mary realized,
for a **school**.

School
in Mary's parlor
began with
her first student,
her stepfather, Thompson,
who had never learned his letters.
One by one
they came,
free and enslaved alike.

All wanted the words
no law could take away.
If caught,
Mary would pay
the fines and fees
for breaking the law.
A fifty-dollar penalty,
some said.
Jail
or twenty lashes, said others.

So Mary's teaching
would need to be kept secret.
Would need to be kept quiet.
They would need
to **keep watch**.

Keeping watch
over the fields,
winds and rain wrestled away
limbs and leaves,
beetles and caterpillars.

Chanterelles and lichen
found harbor as
the MIGHTY OAK
mended,
healed,
nourished,
growing stronger
as seasons passed.

Seasons passed
into years.
Mary found love
in students
who came
quietly,
secretly,
hidden
under night skies,
and left again
secretly,
quietly.

Love found Mary
in a man
named Thomas Peake,
born enslaved,
later freed.
Marriage brought them
a daughter named Harriet.
Daisy, they called her,
blooming bright.

So many
found sanctuary in
Mary's secret schoolhouse,
laboring with their minds
instead of their backs.
They found freedom
in letters.
In Mary's teaching,
they found
a refuge.

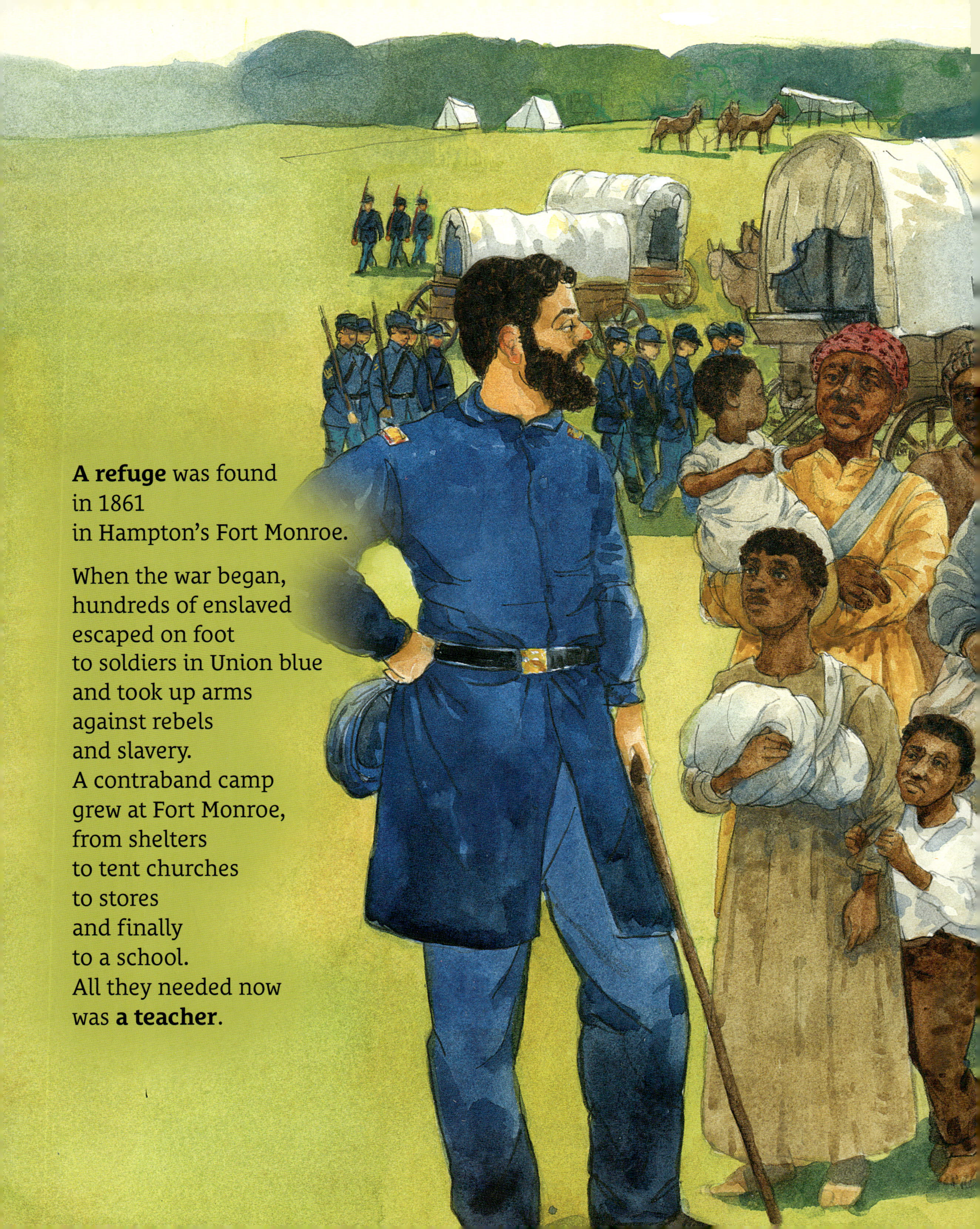

A refuge was found
in 1861
in Hampton's Fort Monroe.

When the war began,
hundreds of enslaved
escaped on foot
to soldiers in Union blue
and took up arms
against rebels
and slavery.
A contraband camp
grew at Fort Monroe,
from shelters
to tent churches
to stores
and finally
to a school.
All they needed now
was **a teacher**.

A teacher
was sought out
by the camp pastor
and the American Missionary Association.
One name,
one teacher
was echoed
throughout the camp:
Mary Peake
Mary Peake
Mary Peake.

Mary Peake's new schoolhouse
was bigger than her parlor,
bigger than a tent.
It held seats
for as many students
as needed.
Under the shade
of a PROUD oak tree,
its branches
flung wide open
like a hug,
waiting,
watching.
Mary began the lesson
to six students the first day,
sixty the next.
Evening skies
brought older students
to sit in the dented grass
where young ones had earlier.
Mary walked among them,
her hands on theirs,
guiding
letters and words and numbers
as a breeze blew softly.

A breeze blew softly
on the whispers of prayers,
Scriptures,
hymns
shared for teacher
Mary Peake.
Lost to illness
in 1862,
she had helped them
to find words
and pride.
Tired and inspired,
they stood
in memory of Mary,
shoulder to shoulder.

Shoulder to shoulder,
all listened
to a soldier in blue
reading a letter
from President Abraham Lincoln.
That on the first day of January, in the year of our Lord one thousand eight hundred and sixty-three, all persons held as slaves within any State . . .
The Emancipation Proclamation
A
STRONG,
PROUD,
MIGHTY tree
blanketed them.
The Emancipation Oak,
they called it,
where seeds were planted
and education
and freedom
took root,
and which in 1868
branched
into *Hampton University*.

A college
built on land
where the oak stands,
proudly watching still.
Students of Mary
educated
season after season
as Mary stood
against fear
and leaned on
My Lord
My Hope
My Trust,
Mary sang aloud
to her students.

Students
built now by a school
that grew them into
teachers
and doctors,
artists
and athletes,
judges
and activists,
politicians
and writers,
ambassadors
and engineers.
All because of an
oak tree
and a
STRONG,
PROUD,
MIGHTY teacher
named Mary Peake.

Photo from the Hampton University Museum Archives

Teacher Mary Peake

Author's Note

Mary Peake's legacy is one that greatly impacted not just the lives of her students, but her legacy has also impacted my own.

I am the daughter of Ernestine Lenora Howard Cline, who was the daughter of Edward Marshall Howard, who began his studies as a student at Hampton University in 1921.

What little I know of my grandfather is revealed in the pictures hung on the walls of my home, in which he poses proudly with his fellow football and basketball teammates from the class of 1924. But I do know that he was the first in his family to attend college at a time when most Black people were denied that opportunity.

Mary Peake, and many other educators like her, was instrumental in creating makeshift classrooms, schoolhouses, and eventually historically Black colleges and universities (HBCUs) and other institutions of higher learning to create educational access for Black people.

The law passed by the Virginia General Assembly in 1831, which made it illegal for Black people to read and write, was just one of many anti-literacy laws passed in the United States in the nineteenth century. Between 1800 and 1835, most Southern states passed laws making it a crime to educate enslaved people. But anti-literacy laws could never completely put a stop to Black people who desperately wanted to learn to read and write. Enslaved Black people continued their quest for literacy, often in secret, even at the risk of punishment, beatings, and death. And when slavery ended, they began opening their own schools.

The largest number of HBCUs began in the years after freedom came. In the year 1867 alone, nine colleges were founded, and that number continued to grow steadily for a century. Today there are 101 historically Black colleges and institutions throughout the country, educating nearly three hundred thousand students each year.

They have produced some of our greatest leaders and notable figures: civil rights leader Reverend Dr. Martin Luther King Jr. (Morehouse College); Vice President Kamala Harris (Howard University); television personality Oprah Winfrey (Tennessee State University); actor Samuel L. Jackson (Morehouse College); Pulitzer Prize–winning author Toni Morrison (Howard University); film director Spike Lee (Morehouse College); writer and poet Langston Hughes (Lincoln University); NASA mathematician Katherine Johnson (West Virginia State University); writer Alice Walker (Spelman College); and tennis champion Althea Gibson (Florida A&M University). And Hampton University alumnus, educator, writer, and leader Booker T. Washington went on to found his own HBCU, Tuskegee University, in 1881.

At over fifty feet tall, the Emancipation Oak is a southern live oak tree whose branches extend to nearly one hundred feet in diameter. Described by the US National Park Service as a "witness tree," or a living historic landmark that has witnessed events throughout history, the two-hundred-year-old oak tree took root in the area that was once home to a community of Indigenous people in the Tsenacommacah region, which the English colonists later renamed Virginia in honor of their queen. The tree has since watched over the Nat Turner Rebellion of 1831 led by a man known as "the Prophet" along with about seventy followers, many of whom were eventually captured or killed; groups of escaping enslaved people settling in Fort Monroe's contraband camps who began fighting with Union troops to defeat Confederate rebels during the Civil War; Mary Peake's death from tuberculosis on February 22, 1862, at thirty-nine years old; the very first Southern reading of the Emancipation Proclamation for which the Black community gathered under the branches of the Emancipation Oak; and the founding of Hampton Institute in 1868 and its designation as a university in 1984.

Before a tiny seed grew into the Emancipation Oak, the land nourished Chief Powhatan uniting and leading many tribes from the Tidewater region along the western shore of the Chesapeake Bay from the 1500s through the early 1600s; colonists from London arriving in 1607 and establishing the Jamestown fort, which displaced the Powhatan people from their ancestral land; the arrival in 1619 of the very first enslaved Africans aboard the *White Lion* at Point Comfort, which later became Fort Monroe; and troops of Revolutionary War soldiers waging a decisive victory in the 1775 fight to gain independence from the British during the Battle of Great Bridge.

The Emancipation Oak still stands today on the campus of Hampton University and is designated as one of the Ten Great Trees of the World by the National Geographic Society.

Photo: iStock.com/XiFotos

The Emancipation Oak on the campus of Hampton University

Edward Marshall Howard, grandfather of the author, as a student and member of the 1924 championship football team at Hampton University in Virginia; seated second row, left

Courtesy of the Hampton University Archives, Hampton, VA